Dear Parent,

Sharing a book is the perfect opportunity to get close and cuddle with your child. Research has shown that reading aloud to and with your child is probably the single most important thing you can do to prepare him or her for success in school. When you share a book with your child, not only are you helping to strengthen his or her reading and vocabulary skills, you are also stimulating your child's curiosity, imagination and enthusiasm for reading.

When Rex accidentally throws Mr Potato Head's ears and nose out of Andy's window, Woody and the gang need to put their heads together to work out how to get them back. Ask your child to think of imaginative 'gadgets' he or she could build to retrieve the items, such as tying dental floss to a toothbrush and using toothpaste for 'glue'. Encourage your child to think in different ways to solve the problem – just like Woody and his friends need to do. Being able to identify with story characters, and think about personal experiences that are similar, is an important strategy that enables readers to more fully understand and engage with the story.

Children learn in different ways and at different speeds. Remember, successful readers have one thing in common: supportive, loving adults who share books with them often, to nurture a lifelong love of books, reading and learning.

Enjoy your reading adventure together!

First published by Parragon in 2012
Parragon
Chartist House
15-17 Trim Street
Bath BA1 1HA, UK
www.parragon.com

Copyright © 2012 Disney/Pixar
Mr. Potato Head® is a registered trademark of Hasbro, Inc. Used with permission.
©Hasbro, Inc. All rights reserved.
Etch A Sketch® ©The Ohio Art Company.
Slinky® Dog is a registered trademark of Poof-Slinky, Inc. ©Poof-Slinky, Inc.

Consultants: Cheryl Stroud, English Language Arts Curriculum Leader and Reading Specialist, Concord Road Elementary School, Ardsley, NY; Beth Sycamore, Literacy Consultant, Chicago, IL

Editor: Joëlle Murphy

Designer: Scott Petrower

Illustrated by the Disney Storybook Artists

All rights reserved. No part of this publication may be reproduced, stored in a retrieval system or transmitted, in any form or by any means, electronic, mechanical, photocopying, recording or otherwise, without the prior permission of the copyright holder.

ISBN 978-1-78186-029-8

Printed in China

Rex Tries to Juggle

Mr Potato Head liked to show off.
"Look at me!" he shouted.
He pulled off his nose.
He pulled off his ears.
Then he threw them into the air.

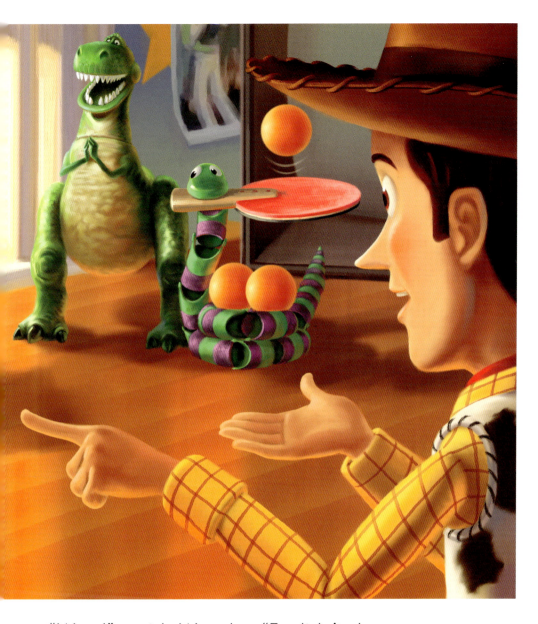

"Wow!" said Woody. "I didn't know you could juggle."

Mr Potato Head put his ears and nose back in place. "I am the best juggler in the toy box!"

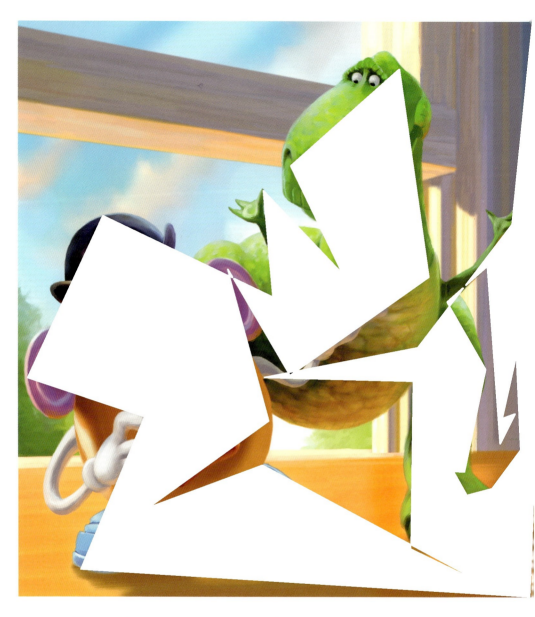

"Can I try?" asked Rex.

Mr Potato Head looked at Rex.
He looked at Rex's short arms.
Rex did not look like he could juggle.

"Here you go," said Mr Potato Head.
He threw his nose and ears over to Rex.

"One, two, three!" shouted Rex.
He threw the nose into the air.
Then he threw the ears.
One, two, three.
The nose and ears went out of the window.

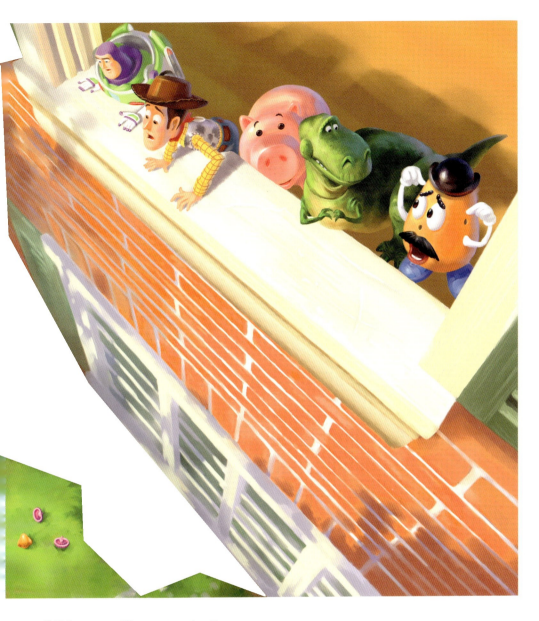

"Oh, no!" cried Rex.

The toys ran to the window.
They looked down.
The nose and ears were in the grass.

"That's just great!" said Mr Potato Head.
"Come get me when you find my nose and ears. I'll be with Snake."

"We must help Rex," said Woody.
"We have to find a way to get down."

Hamm picked up a bandanna.
"I have an idea," said Hamm.
"I can float down on this."

"That will get you down," said Woody.
"But how will you get back up?"

Buzz picked up a ball.
"I have an idea," said Buzz.
"I can bounce down on this."

"That will get you down," said Woody.
"But how will you get back up?"

Rex picked up some toy darts.
"I have an idea," Rex said.
"I can climb down on these."

"That won't work," said Woody.
"The darts won't stick to the brick."

Woody looked at the bandanna.
He looked at the ball and darts.
"I have an idea," said Woody.
"First, tie the bandanna to my lasso."

Woody looked at Rex and Buzz.

"Then, tape the darts to the ball," he said. "Last, loop the end of my lasso around Hamm."

Hamm held the lasso.
Buzz held Hamm.
Rex held Buzz.

Woody sat on the windowsill.
"Now, hold on tight!" Woody shouted.

Down, down, down went Woody.

Hamm held the lasso tight.
"Oh, no!" said Hamm as he looked below.
"The lasso isn't long enough."

Woody looked down.
He saw Mr Potato Head's nose and ears.
They were just below the ball.
Woody knew he could get them.
He had to throw the ball just right.

Woody threw the ball to the ground.
Bounce! Up came Mr Potato Head's nose.
Woody threw the ball again.
Bounce! Up came Mr Potato Head's left ear.
Woody threw the ball one more time.
Bounce! Up came Mr Potato Head's right ear.

"Pull me up!" Woody shouted.
Hamm pulled the lasso.
Buzz pulled Hamm.
Rex pulled Buzz.
Up, up, up went Woody.

"We did it!" shouted Woody.
Hamm took Mr Potato Head's nose.
Rex took Mr Potato Head's ears.
Buzz helped Woody get back inside.

Rex gave Mr Potato Head his ears and nose. "I can't juggle with these," said Rex.

"What could Rex use?" asked Woody.

Woody looked around Andy's room.
He saw Snake playing with some orange ping-pong balls.
"I have an idea," said Woody.
"Get those ping-pong balls," he said to Hamm and Buzz.

Woody looked at Mr Potato Head.
"Can you teach us to juggle
with these?" he asked.

"Yes I can," said Mr Potato Head.
"I *am* the best juggler in the toy box!"

"You go first," Rex said to Woody.
Mr Potato Head gave Woody
the ping-pong balls.

"One, two, three!" shouted Woody.
Oh, no!

Make: A flip book!

Watch Rex juggle! Ask a grown-up to cut out all 16 pages (you'll find more over the page). Next, put the pages in order and staple them together on the left-hand side. Hold the book in your left hand and gently bend the book upwards, allowing the pages to flip from your right hand. For more fun, flip the pages from back to front to see Rex juggle backwards!

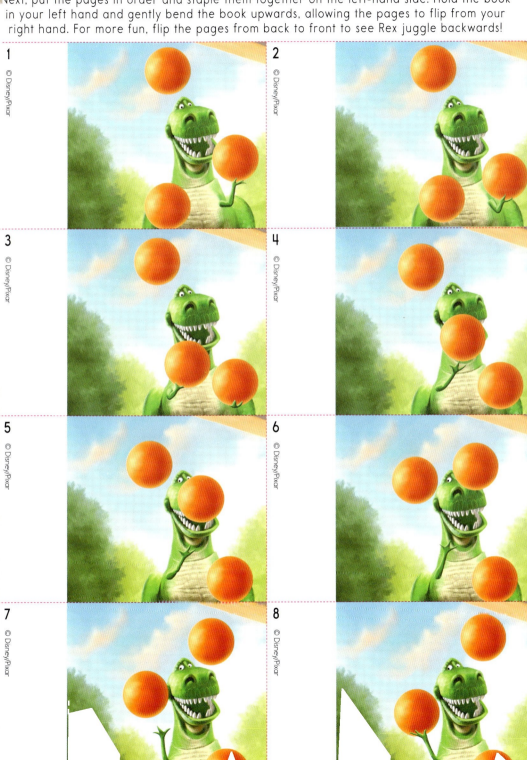

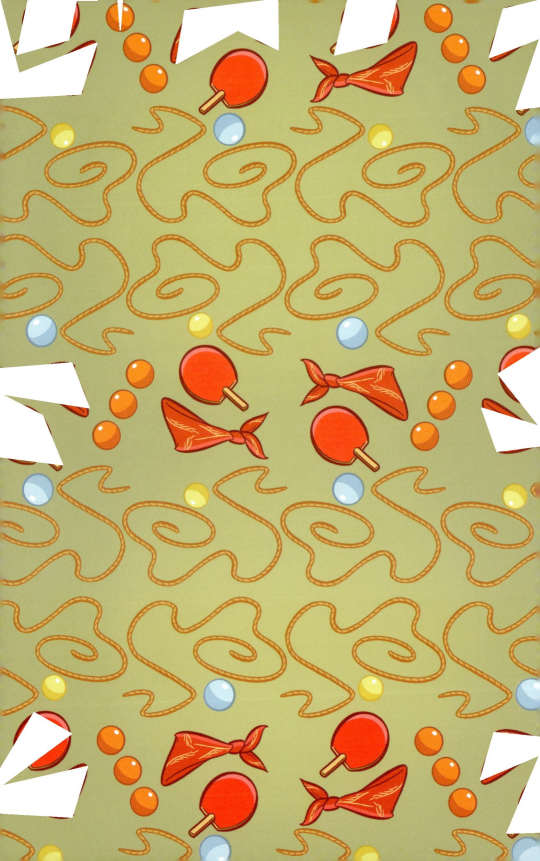

9 © Disney/Pixar

10 © Disney/Pixar

11 © Disney/Pixar

12 © Disney/Pixar

13 © Disney/Pixar

14 © Disney/Pixar

15 © Disney/Pixar

16 © Disney/Pixar

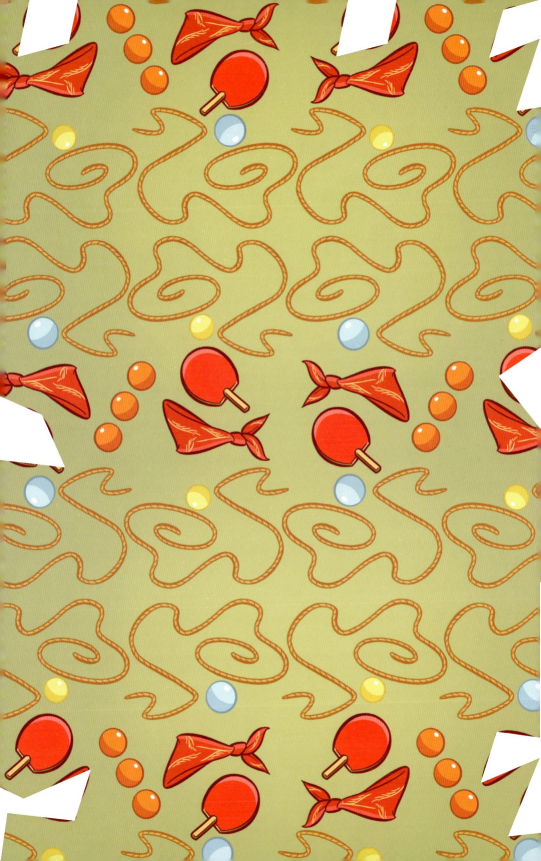

Play: Invent It!
A card game for 2-3 players

Design an invention to rescue Mr Potato Head's parts. The player with the most points at the end of three rounds is the winner!

Set-up
Ask a grown-up to cut out the cards below, following the dotted pink lines. Deal three cards to each player and decide which player will go first. Place the remaining cards in a pile, face down.

Directions continued on the next page.

How to Play

- Each player should look at their cards and decide whether to keep all of them, or exchange up to two cards for new ones. Each card's 'value' is shown by the number of stars it has.
- Players should take it in turns to place their cards face up in front of them. They should then explain how the objects on their cards could work together as a gadget to get Mr Potato Head's parts back into Andy's room.
- Players should keep track of the points they have earned by counting up the number of stars on each of the cards they have used.
- Play a total of three rounds. The player with the highest number of points at the end of three rounds is the winner!